Boundaries
Everybody got
to respect
others
boundaries

Table of contents

B.MY experience with others not respecting my

boundaries

legally

C.Final word

A, Boundaries in human terms

Boundaries in human terms mean legally respecting

others wishes
and privacy;.
Meaning we all
have to respect
someone else's
space ,and their

space could be their home, the inside of it , their wish to be left alone and so on.

Unfortunately in this American society, Some people just do not know how

to respect
others
boundaries due
to their
criminal
intentions, or

mental illness
or just plain
nosiness or
taking the law
into their
hands.

Nosiness is no excuse to violate someone else 's space. However people do it anyway and it causes too many legal problems, - lawsuits, police involvement and unfortunately Peoplehave lost their life due to stalking , and murder which is illegal and violation of someone else's boundaries. Respecting Boundaries in neighborhoods, business and law is essential to people getting along and preventing problems.

B.My experience in dealing with

others not
respecting my
boundaries

When I was
young ,I was
taught to

respect others
when they
want to be left
alone. I was
taught not to
go into a

bathroom where others are showering because they need their space. I was taught that there are laws that protect individuals from being beaten. I

,myself had
these essential
basic common
sense values
tested since I
was young. I

was targeted
by others for
no reason-
harassment,
being beaten
for no good

reason is a sign
of violation of
my boundaries
. I learn to keep
away from bad
people since

those days. Unfortunately more events , I had to face-people stealing things from me

– a violation of
my boundaries
because
stealing is a
crime , theft is
no excuse.; As

an adult ,I had people near me at a home I own gossip about violating the inside of it

to look at me
inside my
bedroom
because they
were
concerned or

nosy- if -that is
true that they
violated my
privacy inside
my home – that
is a crime of

voyeurism , a misdemeanor in the state of California and that is illegal . I suspect it isn't

true and it will
entail legal
actions if it is
true ,and if it is
,that is a
violation of my

constitutional
and legal rights
to expectation
of privacy and
yes! It would
violate my

boundaries. Boundaries are essential- if someone else tell me to stay away ,I have to

,I cannot force myself to keep bothering them , that would not be right. If I break into someone else's home – that would be wrong because it would be criminal trespassing or burglary and yes it would violate someone else's boundaries.

I had dangerous people whom I do not know target me for no good reason

, I told them to keep away but they didn't. That is insane due to their inability to be

civilized and
due to them
not respecting
my boundaries.

C, Final word

Boundaries are

essential to

respecting in

this American

society ,

whether
through love,
home ,etc. It is
what keep us
stable and what

can cause harm

if violated.